International STEAMPUNK FASHIONS

Victoriana Lady Lisa

4880 Lower Valley Road • Atglen, PA 19310

Designed by Danielle D. Farmer
Type set in Vivaldi/Verve/Filosofia

ISBN: 978-0-7643-4207-3
Printed in China

On the front cover (clockwise from top left): Phylida Dolohov, courtesy of NBpix Photographie, France; Photo courtesy of Steampunk Couture, UK; Carlos Jack Winchester, by Adavidphotography. com, Spain; and G.D. Falksen, by photographer Steven Rosen (Stevenrosenphotography.com)

On the back cover (clockwise from top left): Starkall, photography by Rebella Arachnoidea; Catherine Jane Robinson, photography by Viona-Art.com, USA; and G.D. Falksen, photography by Frank Siciliano, USA

On the spine: Emilly Ladybird, aka Jema Hewitt, UK

On the end sheets: Artwork courtesy of In Strict Confidence, Germany

"Clockwork Vertical" © James Steidl. Image from BigStockPhoto.com.
"Ancient Nautical Chart, Grunge" © Artida. Image from BigStockPhoto.com.
"Antique Navigational Chart" © Artida. Image from BigStockPhoto.com.

Published by Schiffer Publishing, Ltd.
4880 Lower Valley Road
Atglen, PA 19310
Phone: (610) 593-1777; Fax: (610) 593-2002
E-mail: Info@schifferbooks.com

For our complete selection of books on this and related subjects, please visit our website at **www.schifferbooks.com.**
You may also write for a free catalog.

This book may be purchased from the publisher.
Please try your bookstore first.

We are always looking for people to write books on new and related subjects. If you have an idea for a book, please contact us at
proposals@schifferbooks.com

Schiffer Publishing's books are available at special discounts for bulk purchases for sales promotions or premiums. Special editions, including personalized covers, corporate imprints, and excerpts can be created in large quantities for special needs.
For more information, contact the publisher.

In Europe, Schiffer books are distributed by
Bushwood Books
6 Marksbury Ave.
Kew Gardens
Surrey TW9 4JF England
Phone: 44 (0) 20 8392 8585; Fax: 44 (0) 20 8392 9876
E-mail: info@bushwoodbooks.co.uk
Website: www.bushwoodbooks.co.uk

Other Schiffer Titles on Related Subjects:

Victorian Decor, 0-7643-1457-2, $59.95
Vintage Victorian Textiles, 0-7643-1504-8, $49.95
Victorian & Edwardian Fashions for Women: 1840–1910, 0-7643-1577-3, $29.95
Victorian Costumes for Ladies, 1860–1900, 2nd Edition, 978-0-7643-3972-1, $29.99
Victorian Fashions for Women and Children: Society's Impact on Dress, 978-0-7643-4164-9, $29.99

This book would not have been possible without the love of my life, John Thomas Grant. His love, guidance, encouragement, and support have been a source of strength for me, not to leave out his photography and technical processing skills, which were necessary to complete this project.

Writing a book has been a dream of mine for at least ten years. During that time I went through some very difficult struggles in a bad marriage. I was finally able to break free and become my own person. Then I met John; he convinced me that I had what it took to write a book and told me that I should fly! He is my greatest friend, confidant, and soulmate; I cherish him every day of my life.

My dearest John, I dedicate this book to you…thanks for believing in me when so many others didn't…look sweetie, I'M FLYING!!!!

All my love, forever and a day…
Your Lisa Ann

Author Victoriana Lady Lisa, photography by John
Thomas Grant, USA

CONTENTS

Top to bottom ✳ Renee Knowles and Joe Mason;
Lord Baron, JCR Vourteque IV;
and Kenzie Kl, courtesy of
Pauldoyle@photographybypaul.com, USA

AUTHOR'S NOTE

It's a privilege for me to have this opportunity to promote so many wonderful and talented photographers, models, designers, artists, entertainers, and musicians in this book. You should all be appreciated for your fine work. Thank you so much to all of those who have contributed!

My goal is to put a book out that depicts the excellent wide range of steampunk fashions worldwide in a positive light, and to give others an opportunity for their talents to be showcased and appreciated.

This book is not all inclusive—I have tried to include as many interpretations of the various unique styles and reach as many countries as possible. I know that there are still many regions out there embracing steampunk around the globe, and it is growing.

I love the Victorian and Edwardian era, having begun collecting antique clothing and accessories at age 15. I adore the fashions and love the steampunk movement because it is keeping the Victorian roots that I am so passionate about alive. Top hats off to the new pioneers of this fantastic movement.

Victoriana Lady Lisa and Kellie LoGrande, photography by John Thomas Grant, USA

Victoriana Lady Lisa, photography by John Thomas Grant, USA

Opposite ✳ Photography and modeling by Pierre Leszczyk EmpireArt, Germany

ACKNOWLEDGMENTS

It has been said by a thousand authors, "Where does one begin to acknowledge all of the many people who have helped shape a book?" I will try my best and if I somehow leave anyone out, my apologies.

As the dedication describes, without the love of my life, John Grant, this book would have never happened; honey, your patience and technical skills were invaluable.

I am grateful to Pete Schiffer and everyone at Schiffer Publishing for giving me this opportunity to share my passion and for their kind, dedicated staff—special thanks to my editor, Jesse Marth.

To my Facebook friends who have played a key part in this book, I thank you. I also thank G.D. Falksen and Evelyn Kriete for being one of the first to answer the call for book submissions. Thank you, Evelyn, for securing some hard to get photos for me. To the many fans, models, photographers, designers, artists, entertainers, and musicians around the world who answered the call for *International Steampunk Fashion* photos, I am truly grateful. This is your book, each and every one that has played a part in it. I only wish that I could have included so many more photos before my deadline. I am amazed and delighted at the incredible talent that I see in the steampunk genre. If your submission did not make the book, it was perhaps due to technical concerns (image file size and resolution), or the required release form was not submitted before the deadline.

Last, but certainly not least, to those who donated their time and finances to get this book up and running and those who lifted me up on the rough days, I thank you with all of my heart. You have encouraged me in more ways than you realize...

Warmest regards,
Victoriana Lady Lisa

Victoriana Lady Lisa and Kellie LoGrande, photography by John Thomas Grant, USA

Gina and Starkall, photography by Pierre Leszczyk
EmpireArt, Germany

G.D. Falksen, photography by Frank Siciliano, USA

engines or the fires industry. Some fans of steampunk may have never read a single work of steampunk fiction, and instead derive their interest in the genre entirely from their connection to the fashion aesthetic.

It must be emphasized that there is nothing wrong with this. While steampunk began in literature, today fashion is at least as prolific a branch of the aesthetic. Indeed, fashion is arguably the strongest and most identifiable part of steampunk. Steampunk clothing can be seen at conventions and events around the world, even those unrelated to the steampunk genre. Photographs of people in steampunk-themed outfits spread around the Internet like wildfire.

What then is steampunk fashion? Perhaps the most straightforward explanation is that it is fashion that could be found in a steampunk book or film. But this explanation relies entirely on steampunk literature as its base, and by now steampunk fashion has a life of its own. It would be more accurate to say that steampunk fashion is fashion inspired by the aesthetics, themes, and styles of the steampunk trend in the same manner that literature, art, film, and music are, each in their own way. And in fashion this is characterized by Victorian era clothing drawn from across the world, made from rich and textured fabric, accented by accessories, and embodying the spirit of a past that might have been but never was.

Steampunk is profoundly aesthetic. From great machines to majestic airships, from smoke-filled factories to the palaces of the mighty, the term "steampunk" conjures up innumerable images of science, industry, grandeur, and wonder. But while steampunk has its origins in literature and has enjoyed ample portrayal in art and film, its most iconic manifestations have, in recent years, been predominately, or even entirely, fashion-oriented. To many, steampunk is as synonymous with corsets, top hats, goggles, and gowns as it is with airships or difference

Steampunk fashion, whether a simple day suit or an elaborate gown, is built from the ground up as an entire piece. It is more than simply slapping gears or goggles onto something and calling it a day. Everything on a steampunk outfit looks like it belongs there, even if it is intended to display extravagance. A steampunk outfit can be simple or complex, loaded with accessories or entirely devoid of them, and it can emulate any social class with equal validity. What matters is that it feels like a cohesive whole, which in turn instills a sense of pride in the wearer and delights the viewer.

Courtesy of Malinda Butson, USA

Evelyn Kriete, photography by Lexmachina, USA

Maurice Grunbaum Redstar, photography by Gillis Michel, France

Why is steampunk fashion so popular? The widespread appeal of steampunk fashion can in part be tied to the general popularity of steampunk, which has been establishing itself as the new big thing for the past five or so years (and that after several earlier years of growth as an artist's movement). But even then, steampunk fashion had its own popularity independent of the larger trend. In the 2007 *New York Times* article on steampunk, the first major media coverage of the trend, fashion was featured prominently and most of the accompanying photographs were fashion shots taken at a New York City outing organized by none other than Evelyn Kriete.

Even before that point, when steampunk took its first real steps into the mainstream, steampunk fashion enjoyed its vogue online. One of the earliest and largest steampunk community sites was the Steamfashion group on Livejournal, which began as a venue for steampunk fans to showcase their outfits. Even before that, other websites and communities not dedicated to steampunk had been used as a place to show photographs of steampunk clothing. Put simply, steampunk fashion has enjoyed a place at the head of the steampunk trend for years and it is not likely to go anywhere soon.

To account for the popularity of steampunk fashion, taken apart from steampunk in general, we must consider the qualities about the style that it cultivates. The first thing that one notices about most steampunk outfits is their attention to detail. And when we say detail, we mean it. Inspired by the Victorian and Edwardian eras, steampunk draws its imagery from a period in history that was fascinated by intricate designs, accessories, and decorative façades. Modern culture has been profoundly affected by the streamlined aesthetics of Modernism in the twentieth century. Clothes today are simple, accessories plain or nonexistent. The aesthetics we see are dominated by the "iPod culture" of today, which endeavors to make things plain, sleek, and identical. Not so with the world that inspires steampunk. Clothes are assembled to fit the wearer, accessories are personalized and made to last, and the name of the game is "individuality." Even when steampunk outfits share a common theme, most are still distinct from one another. And above all, detail reigns. Accessories, embroidery, layers, fabrics, all manner of techniques are used to create texture and enhance the look of the garments.

There is also something to be said about the vintage feel of steampunk fashion. Thanks to art, photography, and film, the clothing of the Victorian era is easy for us to recognize, but it still captures the imagination. It is at once strange and familiar, old and new. This draws many people to steampunk in general, and to steampunk fashion specifically. The fashion style allows people to take Victorian styles and to play with them, to adapt them to personal taste in ways that the Victorians themselves may have been unwilling or unable to do.

Steampunk fashion is both beautiful and fun. It allows people to explore the styles of an earlier time, and to combine them with fantastic ideas drawn from science-fiction. The imagination that is put into the creation of steampunk outfits is truly staggering and anyone, whether a fan or not, can appreciate and enjoy steampunk's many fashion manifestations.

Orla Rose, Creatrix, and Ronxanna Hire, photo by TJ Morgan, photography editing and background digital art created by Orla Rose (Poison-inc.com), USA

STEAMPUNK 101:

By G.D. Falksen

Steampunk Made Quick and Easy

WHAT IS STEAMPUNK?

In three short words, steampunk is Victorian science fiction. Here Victorian is not meant to indicate a specific culture, but rather references a time period and an aesthetic: the industrialized nineteenth century. Historically, this period saw the development of many key aspects of the modern world (mechanized manufacturing, extensive urbanization, telecommunications, office life, and mass-transit), and steampunk uses this existing technology and structure to imagine an even more advanced nineteenth century, often complete with Victorian-inspired wonders like steam-powered aircraft and mechanical computers.

G.D. Falksen,
by photographer Steven Rosen
(Stevenrosenphotography.com)

WHERE DID STEAMPUNK COME FROM?

In some sense, steampunk has existed since the nineteenth century. The Victorian period had its own science fiction, perhaps most famously embodied by the works of Jules Verne and H. G. Wells, and throughout the twentieth century there have been later-day science fiction stories set in the Victorian period. However, the term steampunk was not coined until the late 1980s, when author K. W. Jeter used it humorously to describe

Artwork courtesy of In Strict Confidence, Germany

a grouping of stories set in the Victorian period, written during a time when near-future cyberpunk was the prevailing form of science fiction.

WHERE DOES THE SCI-FI COME IN?

The line between steampunk and period Victorian is extremely narrow, and often the two are indistinguishable. They are separated only by steampunk's status as science fiction, albeit heavily inspired by the historical fact of the Victorian period. This is generally accomplished in one of two ways. The proto steampunk stories of the nineteenth century can be seen as a parallel to our own science fiction: that is, a view of the future from the present. For the Victorians, this meant imagining a future that looks dramatically un-modern to modern eyes. Submarines, space travel, aircraft, and mechanized life were all imagined by the Victorians, but while some of these came very close to the mark, they still differed from where the future actually went. For modern writers, with the benefit of modern science, steampunk becomes a re-imagining of the nineteenth century with a view of where science will one day go. In this way, steampunk often works to translate modern concepts such as the computer revolution, spy thrillers, noir mysteries, and even the Internet into a Victorian context using Victorian technology. Steampunk becomes the perfect blending of alternate history and science fiction.

WHERE DOES THE STEAM COME IN?

Nina Covington in Oracle Of LoFi, by photographer Thomas Dodd, USA

Steampunk's steam references more than simply the technology itself, although steam engines are a vital aspect of life in a steampunk world. Steam more generally signifies a world in which steam technology is both dominant and prolific. During the Victorian era, steam power revolutionized almost every aspect of life. The steam engine made full-scale industrialization possible and replaced human and animal labor as the basic unit of energy production. Mechanized manufacturing and farming caused an upheaval in the structure of working life, but they dramatically increased society's productivity and freed up an entire section of society to form the modern class of professionals and office workers. The changes in society brought on by steam-driven industrialization allowed for the unprecedented developments in sciences, society, and goods that came to be associated with the Victorian era. Steampunk takes inspiration from these changes and applies them to whatever culture it influences.

WHERE DOES THE PUNK COME IN?

Courtesy of BB BlackDog, photography by Terry Godwin, UK

Ironically, it doesn't. As was mentioned earlier, the term steampunk is a tongue in cheek reference to the cyberpunk genre rather than a reference to the punk subculture. Moreover, punk in the context of punk rock was the product of very specific circumstances following World War II, which makes it fundamentally distinct from the Victorian aesthetic that inspires steampunk. However, individuals interested in exploring a steampunk equivalent to twentieth century punk can find a wealth of material in nineteenth century counterculture groups ranging from the Luddites to

Courtesy of www.facebook.com/Micky. Artworld, photography Warped-prod.com, France

utopians to hooligans. Add a dash of Victorian street culture and a sprinkling of ragtime, and steampunk punk comes into focus.

WHAT ABOUT GEARS?

The gear is an easily recognized symbol of steampunk, but it is not unique to the genre. It was invented long before the nineteenth century and it remains in use today. The gear in steampunk joins related devices such as flywheels and pistons as the "power lines" of the steam age. Steam power is mechanical power and its transmission demands a network of moving parts in the same way that electrical power transmission demands wires. The gear on its own is not especially steampunk but when put to use in nineteenth century machinery, it becomes a key icon of the genre.

WHAT ABOUT GOGGLES?

Goggles are often encountered in steampunk clothing and imagery, and this can create the misleading impression that they are somehow fundamental to the steampunk look. Certainly, goggles are associated with both science and mechanized travel, both of which are common themes in steampunk. However, this does not mean that everyone in a steampunk setting wears goggles; in fact, only people who have a reason to wear them do so, and then only while it is useful. As with scarves, driving coats, aprons, and overalls, goggles are a piece of fashion that can help give life to a steampunk world when used properly and in moderation, but can rapidly border upon the ludicrous when turned into an end rather than a means.

The Wycliffe Ocular Assembly Mk2 by Mark Cordory Creations, UK

WHAT IS THE APPEAL OF STEAMPUNK?

A genre as large as steampunk has a wide-ranging appeal. Some people are drawn to it from a love of the Victorian period. Others enjoy steampunk's unique approach to technology: re-imagining modern capabilities with nineteenth century machines. Many people are drawn to it in light of its fashion aspects, which allow them to sample and even combine a range of clothing styles and accessories from across the nineteenth-century world. One critical aspect of steampunk is the tremendous diversity of appeal it presents, which allows it to offer something for just about everyone. Steampunk is also aided by a more general neo-vintage movement, which has been steadily progressing through mainstream fashion, film, and aesthetics, but even this cannot wholly explain steampunk's appeal. The genre possesses a life of its own that draws in fans from countless directions and backgrounds into a world where fashion is tailored to the individual, goods are made to last, and machinery is still regarded as a thing of visual majesty.

STEAMPUNK SOUNDS GREAT! WHERE'S AN EASY PLACE TO START?

The basic rule of thumb for steampunk is start period and then add. One of steampunk's great advantages is that the period it is inspired by, the Victorian era, saw the invention of photography and cinematic film. These in turn allowed for a visual record of people

Catherine Jane Robinson, photography by Viona-Art.com, USA

from all different classes, cultures, and backgrounds, providing an unprecedented amount of reference material. People looking for fashion ideas, character inspirations, or scenes to describe can find a wealth of starting points in the countless vintage photographs and film reels left over from the nineteenth century.

All that remains is to add to or modify the depictions to taste, though it must be remembered that many aspects of a steampunk world and its people will likely remain virtually indistinguishable from the period that inspires them.

INTRODUCTION

Welcome to International Steampunk Fashions

WHAT'S OLD IS NEW AGAIN!

In the nineteenth century, among the well to do in society, it was of the utmost importance to be seen, and to be seen well. There were utilitarian clothes for the common folk who generally could not escape their station in life. Then there was clothing for the pure sake of fashion. Oh the beauty of it! A favorite neo-Victorian style is an extraordinary fashion trend called steampunk. What is steampunk you ask? It began as a literary movement, and as people began to meet, they assembled imaginative outfits and accessories to complement the fantasy. Imagine the styles of the steam locomotive era along with a modern twist if you will. There is a lot of debate about what is and isn't steampunk fashion. I concur that if it has any roots in the era of steam travel, then it is considered steampunk. It's a sort of fashion fantasy, what the Victorians would have worn back then if they had access to our modern inventions, a back-to-the-future marriage of style. One of the things that I love about steampunk is the aspect of individuality in one's ensemble. There are some basics to the look such as the explorer, the inventor, and the traditionalist, but then personal style takes over in a most marvelous manner. As a Victorian historian and re-enactor, I adore wearing the traditional corset style with touches of modern steampunk accessories. Whatever your preference, there really is no wrong way to express yourself. The fashion connects us and allows us a sense of belonging with our peers in this genre. Dare I say a historical futuristic family of those who simply want to have a good time among friends?

We are such a disposable, fast paced society that many of us crave more simplicity and durability in our lives. We harken back to a time in history where things were savored, craftsmen and inventors were revered, and things were proudly made to last. There are many excellent designers and purveyors for steampunk fashion today, many of their wonderful photos will be seen among the pages in this book.

In the nineteenth century, women's fashions were proper, feminine, and subtly sensual in a way that still enamors many of us

Ember Lark, courtesy of Insomniac Studios, St. Louis, MO, USA

Ami Sprandel, courtesy of Insomniac Studios, St. Louis, MO, USA

today. The hourglass shape of the corset was and is still titillating. The crinoline, bustle, and many-layered petticoats concealed, yet promised unseen delights. Just the glimpse of a woman's ankle would drive a man crazy in the day.

Women's steampunk fashions now can include corsets worn on the *outside*, bustle dresses, top hats, capes and cropped jackets, lace gloves, ornate cuffs, flounced skirts, ruffled tops, lace up boots, aviator glasses, parasols, parachute pants, and much more. There is a touch of traditional Victorian influence with a futuristic eye for style.

Gina and Starkall, photography by Pierre Leszczyk EmpireArt, Germany

Men's fashions in the nineteenth century were proper and dignified. Today gents wear waistcoats, tails, vests, top hats, bowler hats, aviator style jackets and pants, goggles, arm bands, jodhpurs, and pocket watches, just to name a few. The influence of time travel, inventions, and fully charged futuristic weapons can be detected. Many women also adopt this style as their own—anything goes!

Steampunk jewelry is another fabulous way to accessorize the look; everything from bracelets to chokers to brooches are made from broken watch parts, chains, beads, lace, antique keys, cameo pieces, and other small mechanical items. The possibilities are as endless as the designer's imagination.

The Fenwick Temporal Chronometer Mk1 by Mark Cordory Creations, UK

Having received incredible photos of steampunk fashions from fans all over the world, this book was born. Showcased among these pages for your delight are the talents of many. We owe it to our ancestors and the pioneers of the Industrial Revolution to keep their memory alive, whether by invention or fashion. In steampunk we have the rich beauty of combing both.

Johan Rydberg crafts and steampunk aeronaut Pontus Karlsson, Sweden

Chapter 1
EUROPE

Photography by Starkall, model Rachael Forbes at Manor Ecclescreig, Scotland

Phylida Dolohov, courtesy of
NBpix Photographie, France

Emilly Ladybird, aka Jema Hewitt, UK

Kato, courtesy of
Steampunk Couture, UK

Gina, photography courtesy of Pierre Leszczyk EmpireArt, Germany

Courtesy of In Strict Confidence, Germany

Andy Heintz & The Men
That Will Not Be Blamed For
Nothing with model Tears of
Envy, photography courtesy of
T.P. Sutton (Facebook.com/
blamedfornothing), UK

Courtesy of Mark Lancaster, UK

Simona V Vinati, photography by Paola Verde, Germany

23

Elizabeth Winchester, by
Adavidphotography.com, Spain

Carlos Jack Winchester, by
Adavidphotography.com, Spain

Rebella Fiendish, photography by
Pierre Leszczyk EmpireArt. Germany

Johan Rydberg, steampunk monsterologist, Sweden

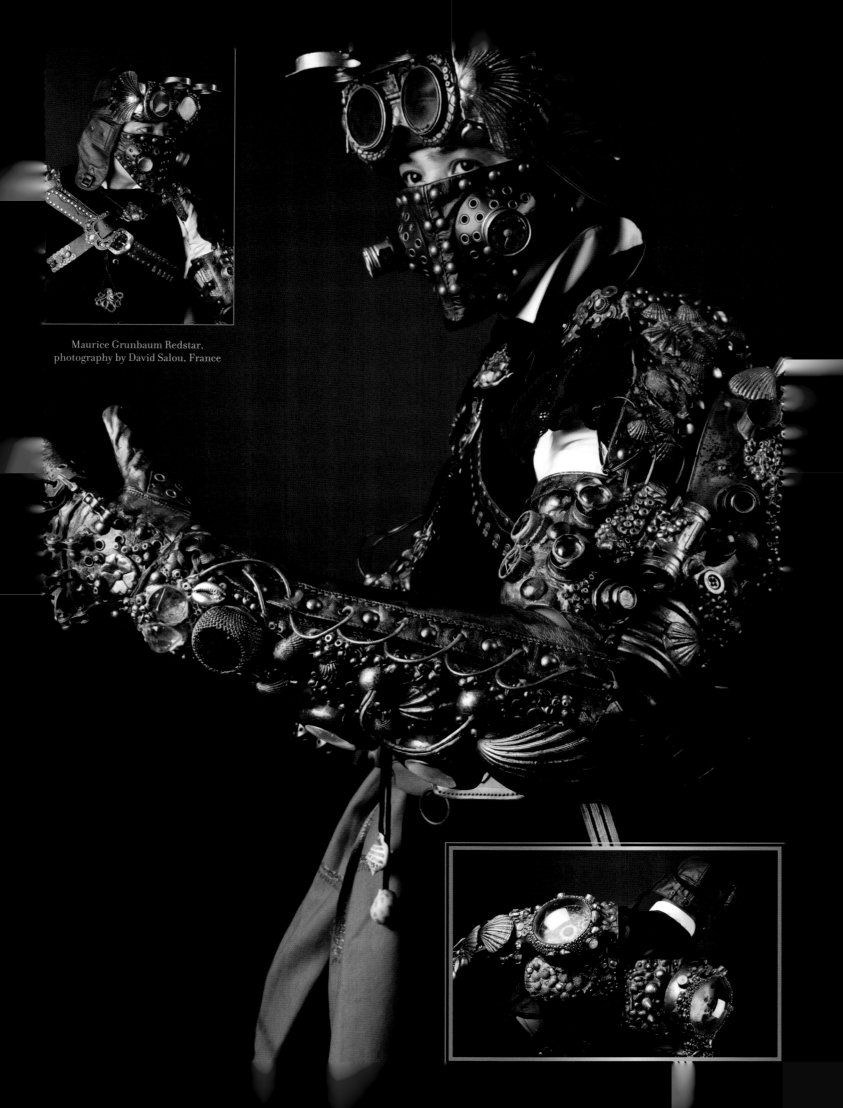

Maurice Grunbaum Redstar,
photography by David Salou, France

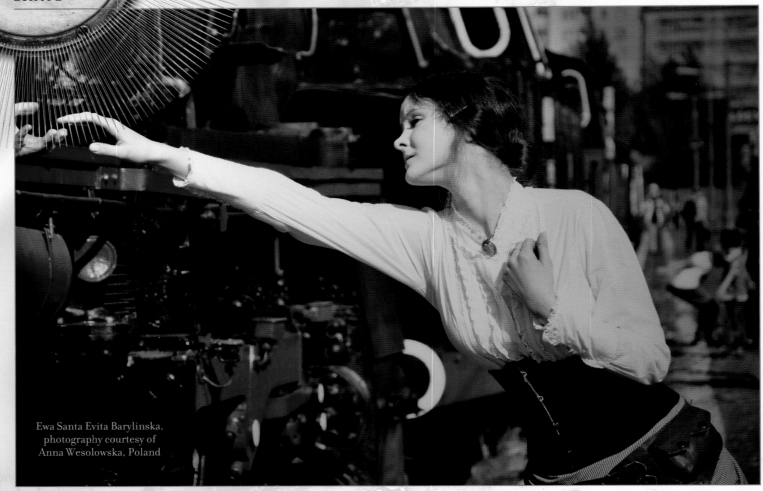

Ewa Santa Evita Barylinska.
photography courtesy of
Anna Wesolowska, Poland

Phylida Dolohov, courtesy of NBpix
Photographie, France

Melusine, photography courtesy of
Pierre Leszczyk EmpireArt, Germany

Marion Andre, photography by Chateauvieux-Sebastien, France

Top right ✳ Courtesy of Agata Bottoni, Italy

Bottom right ✳ Marion Andre, photography by Chateauvieux-Sebastien, France

Photography by Starkall, models
Markus Spatzier and Ophelia
Overdose at Preußen Punk Picnic
2010, Leipzig, Germany

Jema Hewitt,
aka Emilly
Ladybird,
as Absinthe
Fairy, UK

Rebella Fiendish photography by Pierre Leszczyk EmpireArt, Germany

New Steam by artist Laurent Celsy, Belgium

Phylida Dolohov, courtesy of NBpix
Photographie, France

Elizabeth Winchester, by Adavidphotography.com, Spain

Aidenn Queen,
photography courtesy of
Pierre Leszczyk
EmpireArt, Germany

www.SteampunkItalia.com, photography by Serenella Volpe, Italy

Ladon,
photography
courtesy of
Pierre Leszczyk
EmpireArt,
Germany

Ewa Santa Evita Barylinska,
courtesy of Caradelneil, Poland

Knut Stanley Jacobsen,
photography by Tore Hanson, Netherlands

www.SteampunkItalia.com, photography by
Serenella Volpe, Italy

Izumihiiiflower at the Eiffel Tower, photography by
Michel Gillis, France

Maan Limburg, photography by
Pierre Leszczyk EmpireArt, Germany

Detail of bodice on Lyssa Ryan, photo
by Mart Soulstealer, UK
(Soulstealer.co.uk)

Lyssa & Leo Ryan, photography by
Mart Soulstealer, UK (Soulstealer.co.uk)

Starkall and Gina,
photography by Pierre Leszczyk
EmpireArt, Germany

www.SteampunkItalia.com,
photography by Serenella Volpe, Italy

Phylida Dolohov, courtesy of NBpix Photographie, France

Lise Gustafson and Beate Bertehussen, photography by Gregor McNeil, Norway

Mr. Tib, courtesy of facebook.com/Mickey.Artworld,
photography Warped-prod.com, France

Sorsha, taken by Dan Clay photography (catalystphotography@hotmail.co.uk), UK

47

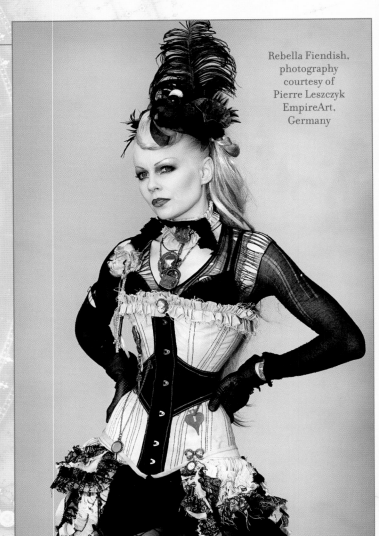

Rebella Fiendish,
photography
courtesy of
Pierre Leszczyk
EmpireArt,
Germany

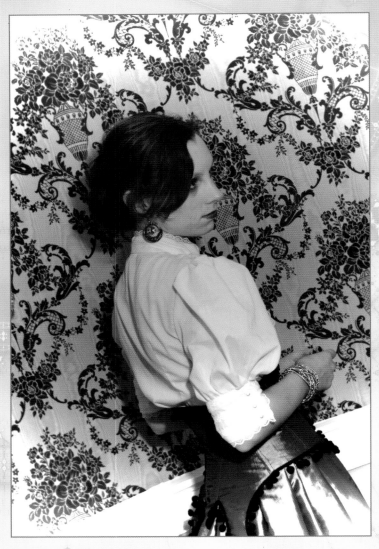

Joanna Read (Blueladycouture.co.uk), photography by Scott Read
(Scott.read@imp-net.co.uk), UK

Ranato Guerrucci, photography
courtesy of Agata Bottoni, Italy

Maan Limburg and Kevin
Timmerman, designs by Rosie's
Art, photography by Pierre Leszczyk
EmpireArt, Germany

Julien Frontil, photography by
Gilles Michel, France

49

Ophelia Overdose, photography courtesy of
Pierre Leszczyk EmpireArt, Germany

Federico Sinoncini, photography courtesy of Agata Bottoni, Italy

Kevin Timmerman, photography by Pierre Leszczyk EmpireArt, Germany

Camilo Marq, My Lord Octopus, at the Eiffel Tower, photography by Gillis Michel, France

Marion Andre and Kris Sobry at the Eiffel Tower,
photography by Gillis Michel, France

Kris Sobry at the Eiffel Tower,
photography by Gillis Michel, France

www.SteampunkItalia.com, photography by Serenella Volpe, Italy

Genevieve, photo courtesy
of Steampunk Couture, UK

Sorsha, taken by Dan Clay photography
(catalystphotography@hotmail.co.uk), UK

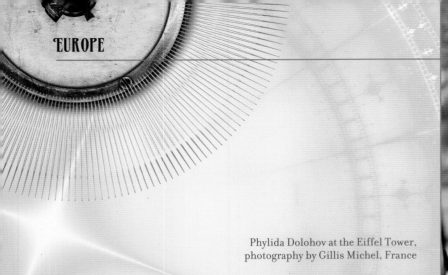

Phylida Dolohov at the Eiffel Tower, photography by Gillis Michel, France

Photo courtesy of Steampunk Couture, UK

Katerina, by Lina Kara, Rag Dollies Madhouse, Greece

Courtesy of NBpix Photographie, France

Gina & Markus Spatzier, fashions by Herzblutcouture
by M. Spatzier, photography courtesy of Pierre
Leszczyk EmpireArt, Germany

59

Ulorin Desert,
photo courtesy
of Steampunk
Couture, UK

Photo courtesy of Steampunk Couture, UK

Courtesy of NBpix
Photographie,
France

Professor Maelstromme, photography by Mart Soulstealer, UK (Soulstealer.co.uk)

Liam Murray Steampunk Overload, UK, photography by Mart Soulstealer (Soulstealer.co.uk)

Cecile Dubuis, photography by Mart Soulstealer, UK (Soulstealer.co.uk)

Lady Georgina Marsh, photography by Mart
Soulstealer, UK (Soulstealer.co.uk)

SteamDoll, by artist
Laurnet Celsy, Belgium

The Rawlinson Patented Psychic Analysis Engine
Mk by Mark Cordory Creations, UK

Tim Burton wedding gown, designed by Jema Hewitt, aka Emilly Ladybird, UK

Artwork by Mary M. Tarkoff

Courtesy of Bernard Rousseau, France

Suzie Jubb, Maurice Jubb, Trevor Wilson, and Jackie Wilson, photography courtesy of Mart Soulstealer, UK (Soulstealer.co.uk)

Steampunk picnic, courtesy of Bernard Roussaeu, France

Bounty Hunter and Adventurer Explorer, designed by Dave and modeled by Jo Aitken. photography by Neave R. Willoughby

Anna Key, aka Nathalee Taylor, Safe Keeper of the Keys of the Universe, winner of the children's category, 2011 Oamaru Steampunk Fashion Show, New Zealand, photography by Neave R. Willoughby

Anzhela, Princess and Philanthropic Adventurer, designed by Ros
Merridan and modeled by Rebecca Dennison, Oamaru Steampunk
Fashion Show, New Zealand, photography by Neave R. Willoughby

Rose the Automated Wife, designed by Richard McWha,
Supreme Winner, 2011 Oamaru Steampunk Fashion Show,
New Zealand, photography by Neave R. Willoughby

Lady Flo Tinnaway, aka Leanne Parkingson, Explorer of Noble Birth, Oamaru
Steampunk Fashion Show, New Zealand, photography by Neave R. Willoughby

Rose the Automated Wife, designed by Richard McWha,
Supreme Winner, 2011 Oamaru Steampunk Fashion Show,
New Zealand, photography by Neave R. Willoughby

Chapter 3
NORTH & SOUTH AMERICA

Kellie LoGrande, photography by John Thomas Grant, USA

Kellie LoGrande and Victoriana Lady Lisa, photography by John Thomas Grant, USA

Steamgirl, by artist Josh Stebbins, USA

Orla Rose, photography by Scott Speck (ScottSpeck.com), USA

Jacqueline Ann Bunge,
courtesy of M. Haight
Photography, USA

Jerry Abuan, photography courtesy of JerryAbuan.Zenfolio.com, USA

Courtesy of Joan V., alternative model, Canada

Cindy Piselli, photography courtesy of JerryAbuan.Zenfolio.com, USA

Sherri Terryne Rose-Washington shot at
Tybee Island, GA, by Dortch Designs: Anthony
Dortch, creative director; Lisa Simser,
photographer; Anthony Canney, fashion
designer; Time Cabell, hair and makeup; and
Inez Del Tufo, makeup, USA

Sherri Terryne Rose-Washington shot at Tybee
Island, GA, by Dortch Designs: Anthony Dortch,
creative director; Lisa Simser, photographer;
Anthony Canney, fashion designer; Time Cabell,
hair and makeup; and Inez Del Tufo, makeup, USA

Orla Rose (Poison-inc.com), photo by Ren Garczynski at
Random Eye Candy Photography, USA

Kellie LoGrande
wearing a jacket by
Clockwork Couture,
photography by
John Thomas Grant,
USA

Courtesy of Michael Salerno, USA

Steamgirl in red sepia, by artist
Josh Stebbins, USA

Steampunk Felicity, by Steampunk Threads, USA

Alisha, courtesy of Ray Feather Photography, USA

Courtesy Joan V., alternative model, Canada

Photography and
model by Hatton Cross
Steampunk, USA

81

Stephanie Peregrinis, by Freak Altenative Photographics, USA

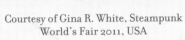

Courtesy of Gina R. White, Steampunk
World's Fair 2011, USA

Phil Powell, by photographer Steven Rosen
(Stevenrosenphotography.com)

Astra Crompton. photography by Geoectomy Photography, British Columbia

Cherie Savoie, wings by Ryan Smith, fashions by Amber Calderilla, photo courtesy of JerryAbuan.Zenfolio.com, USA

Aleister Kidd, photography by Pongo, USA

Deux Ciseaux, model: Devin Faith, photography by Cherie Savoie, USA

Mawson Made, by photographer John T. Riley, USA

Scottozoid Art & Salvage, photography by Dennis The Wolfe Totin, USA

Nox Artemis, photographed by
Jessica Martin, USA

Emmy Jackson in Last Wear Clothing & Gypsy Lady hat,
photography by Lex Machina, USA

Jacqueline Ann Bunge, courtesy of
M. Haight Photography, USA

Jacqueline Ann Bunge, courtesy of
M. Haight Photography, USA

Carrie Meyer, photography by
John T. Riley, USA

Astra Crompton, aka Madame Gunslinger,
photography by Glennis Taylor, British Columbia, Canada

Vanessa Wood, photography by
JerryAbuan.Zenfolio.com, USA

Photo courtesy of Beth Carson, USA

Left ✷ Courtesy of Gina Walters White, USA

Courtesy of model Dr. Brassy Steamington, USA

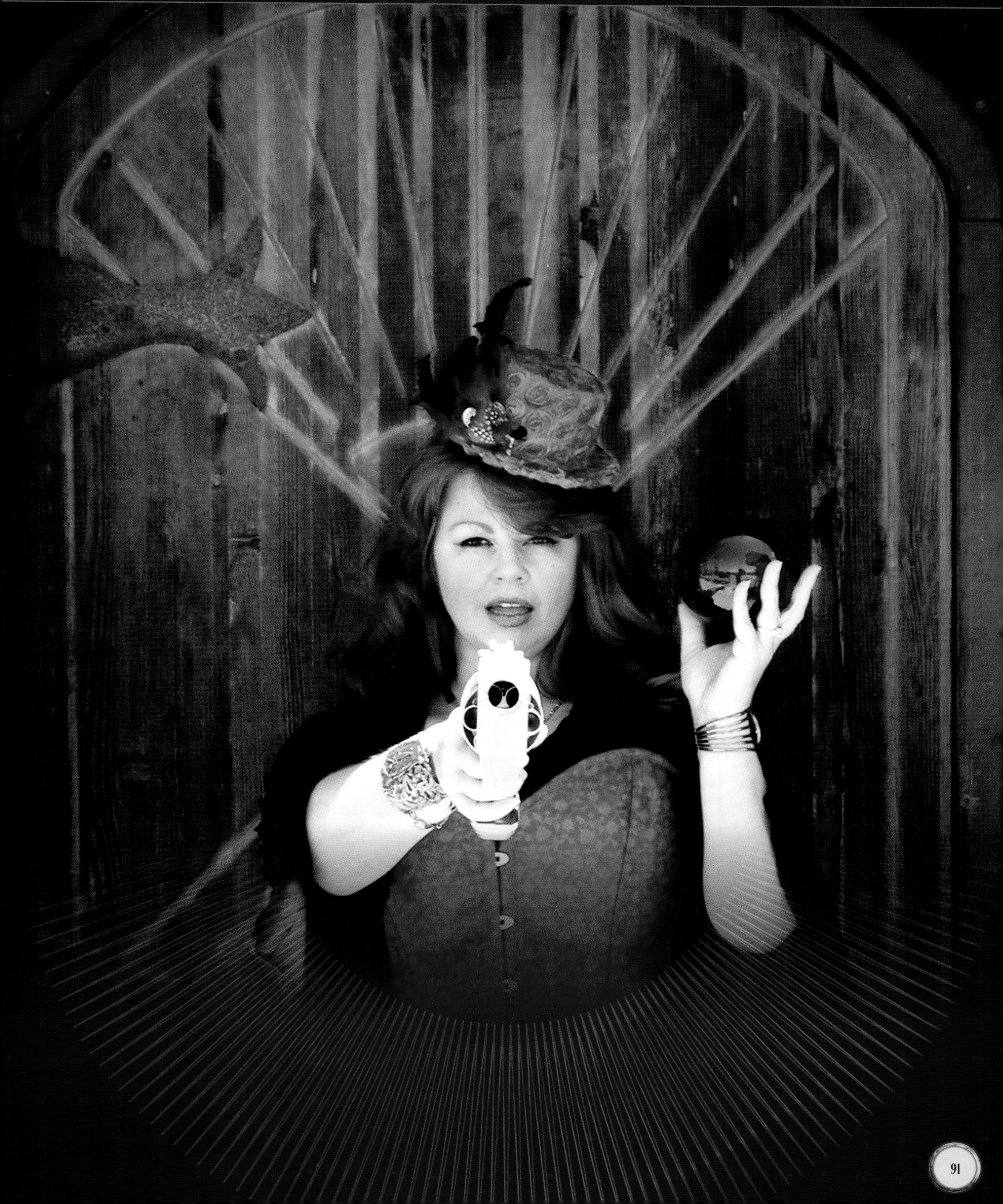

Courtesy of Malinda
Butson, USA

Steampunk Lisa, aka Victoriana Lady, by artist
Josh Stebbins, USA

Courtesy of Steven
Chapman, USA

Mark Rosenqvist, photography courtesy of Pamela Rosenqvist, USA

Courtesy Photographic
Service International
2011, USA

Airship Pilot S L Medina, by Cherie Savoie, USA

Monique Elwell, by Jema Hewitt, aka Emilly Ladybird, USA

Goszleth I.

BUDAPEST
Kristof-tér 3 sz.

Joan V., MUA Poison
I-V D'Monique at The
Princess Street Antiques
Village Market, Winnipeg,
Manitoba, Canada, photo
by AilsaDyson.com
Photography

Sarah, by Russ Turner Photography, USA

Kristen Deceder, by Ray Feather
Photography, USA

Artwork for the privileged series, by Anthony Dortch, 8x10 mixed media,
May 2011, Anthony Canney fashion designer for dress, USA

Astra Crompton,
photography
by Geoectomy
Photography,
British Columbia

Joana Sharp,
photography by
Cherie Savoie,
USA

Courtesy of Gina
White at Steampunk
World's Fair 2011

Vanessa Wood, photography by JerryAbuan.Zenfolio.com, USA

Vanessa Wood's stockings, by
JerryAbuan.Zenfolio.com, USA

Jacqueline Ann Bunge, courtesy of M. Haight Photography, USA

Jerry Abuan, photography courtesy of JerryAbuan.Zenfolio.com, USA

Cindy Lee, photography by Christa Ickowski, USA

Alexandra Ofstedahl, photography by Cherie Savoie, USA

Photography courtesy of
model Rose Wollack

Courtesy of Malinda Butson, USA

Jacqueline Ann Bunge, courtesy of M. Haight Photography, USA

Rose Tursi & Ryan Neal, photography by Cherie Savoie, USA

Orla Rose
(Poison-inc.com),
photo by
Ren Garczynski
at Random
Eye Candy
Photography, USA

Stephanie Peregrinis, by
Freak Altenative Photographics, USA

Alisha, courtesy of
Ray Feather Photography, USA

Steamgirl 2 by Josh
Stebbins, USA

Natälie, by Russ Turner
Photography, USA

Joan V. & Lou Valcourt, MUA
Poison I-V D'Monique at
The Princess Street Antiques
Village Market in Winnipeg,
Manitoba, Canada, photos by
AilsaDyson.com Photography

Ashley, photography by Paul Esquer, USA

Photography and
model by Hatton
Cross Steampunk,
USA

Photography and model by Hatton
Cross Steampunk, USA

Photo courtesy of
Beth Carson, USA

Photo courtesy of
Marissa Marinello,
USA

Le Guepe, by photographer Cherie C
Savoie, hair by Dan Van Clapp, USA

Photography and model by Hatton Cross Steampunk, USA

Ember Lark, courtesy of Insomniac
Studios, St. Louis, MO, USA

Realistic, by photographer Cherie Savoie, USA

Astra Crompton, by Geoectomy Photography, British Columbia

Jacqueline Ann Bunge, photography courtesy of M. Haight Photography, USA

Crystal Taylor, aka Moxie
Macabre, in Retroscope Fashions,
photography by Kit Rogers, USA

Courtesy of Joan V.,
alternative model, Canada

Ashley,
photography by
Paul Esquer

Anabel of the Ball, wearing
Retroscope Fashions, USA

Lee Ann Faruga
and family, by
Brigid Ashwood.
Canada

Ashley, photography by Paul Esquer

Courtesy of
Ray Feather
Photography,
USA

Victoriana Lady
Lisa, photography
by John Thomas
Grant, USA

Astra Crompton,
aka Professor Skylar Raynes,
photographed by Geoectomy,
British Columbia, Canada

Kelly, by Russ Turner
Photography, USA

Kimber Lee, fashions
by Anthony Canney,
photography by
Thomas Dodd, USA

Kellie LoGrande.
photography by John
Thomas Grant. USA

Normandie. by Steampunk Threads. USA

Jacqueline Ann
Bunge, courtesy
of M. Haight
Photography, USA

Circle ✳ Courtesy of model
Dr. Brassy Steamington, USA

Victoriana Lady Lisa,
Photography by John
Thomas Grant

Courtesy of Gina Walters White, USA

Gretchen Jacobson, aka Wilhelmina Frame Editrix de Mode,
SteampunkChronicle.com, photo by Mary Lesh, USA

Jacqueline Ann Bunge.
photography courtesy of
M. Haight Photography. USA

Model and fashion designer Leah D'Andre, photography by Oleg Volk (Volkstudio.com)

Courtesy of
Jonathan Ibarra

Courtesy of
Jonathan Ibarra

Rocio Caro Casanueva, by Juan Carlos Avila, Chile

Chapter 4

JEWELRY, HATS, AND ACCESSORIES

Antique clocks and watches, author's collection, USA

Her World design courtesy of Turner's Tokens, USA

Something-old-something-new, designed by
Jema Hewitt, aka Emilly Ladybird, UK

Clockwork garden bracelet, designed by
Jema Hewitt, aka Emilly Ladybird, UK

Guantini collage, courtesy of Agata Bottoni, Italy

Design
by Rag
Dollies
Madhouse,
Lina Kara,
Greece

Designs courtesy of MacMcGowan/Steambaby.net

125

Cecile Dubuis, photography by Mart
Soulstealer, UK (Soulstealer.co.uk)

Steampunk bracelet with unusual antique pocket watch movement by Daniel Proulx of Catherinette Rings, USA

Design by Marija Jillings of Jazz Steampunk, Netherlands

Design by Marija Jillings of Jazz Steampunk, Netherlands

Wasp brooch design by Denise Humphrey, UK

Bumble Bee brooch design by Denise
Humphrey, UK

Design by Rag Dollies Madhouse, Lina Kara, Greece

Design by
Rag Dollies
Madhouse, Lina
Kara, Greece

Jollyroger and Ruddy David, photography by Bernard Rousseau, France

Orla Rose, photo by TJ Morgan, photo editing and background digital art created by Orla Rose (Poison-inc.com), USA

Courtesy Valentine Roy-Connell,
Vee Cee Design Co., Canada

Design courtesy of Mirzhin Creation, France

Hallmark of the Baldrick, designed by The Steampunk Surplus, photography by Gary Lobstein-Day 304., USA

G.E.A.R. Ambassador's Regalia, Scoria Prefecture, designed by The Steampunk Surplus, photography by Gary Lobstein-Day 304, USA

Pendant courtesy of Valentine Roy-Connell, Vee Cee Design Co., Canada

Antique brooch, author's collection, USA

Design by Elease Sinister Vanity, USA

Courtesy of model Dr. Brassy Steamington (etsy.com/shop/DrBrassySteampunk), USA

Pendant design by Elease Sinister Vanity, USA

Design by Marija Jillings of Jazz Steampunk, Netherlands

Design by Marija Jillings at Jazz Steampunk, Netherlands

Design by Rag Dollies Madhouse, Lina Kara, Greece

Design by Rag Dollies Madhouse, Lina Kara, Greece

Filigree Flowers Necklace
by Anna Murfin, USA

Cognatise Matching Jewelry Set by
Anna Murfin, USA

138

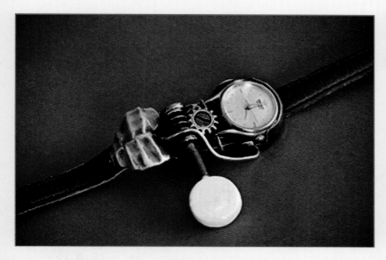

Watch design courtesy of Ivan Mavrovic, Croatia

Watch design courtesy of Ivan Mavrovic, Croatia

House Hanover Service Medallion, designed by The Steampunk Surplus, photography by Gary Lobstein-Day 304, USA

Design by Turner's Tokens, USA

Bird Necklace, designed
by Amy Brillion, USA

Maurice Grunbaum Redstar,
photography by David Salou, France

Spider earrings design by Denise Humphrey, UK

Heart brooch design by Denise Humphrey, UK

Atlantis necklace, designed by Jema Hewitt,
aka Emilly Ladybird, UK

Clockwork heart necklace, designed by Jema Hewitt,
aka Emilly Ladybird UK

Jungle earrings, designed by Jema Hewitt, aka Emilly Ladybird, UK

Design by Jennifer Ramirez, USA

Design by Jennifer Ramirez, USA

Phantasmagoriallibration devices,
designed by Jema Hewitt, aka
Emilly Ladybird, UK

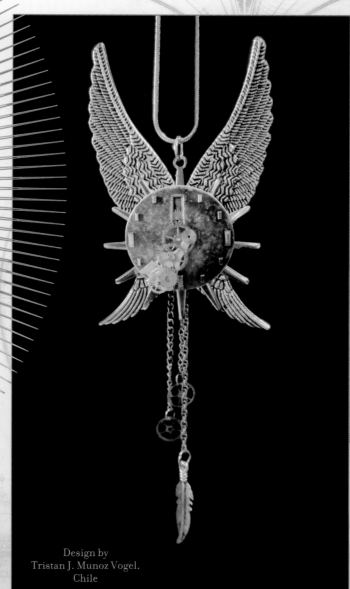

Design by
Tristan J. Munoz Vogel,
Chile

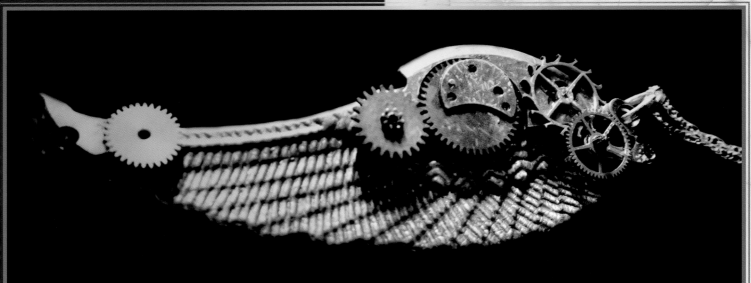

Design by Tristan J. Munoz Vogel, Chile

Opposite ✳ Liz Burgess, photography
by Shelley Shearer, USA

Designs by Rag Dollies Madhouse,
Lina Kara, Greece

Eyes Like Clockwork design courtesy of Turner's Tokens, USA

Bruised but Not Broken
design courtesy of Turner's
Tokens, USA

Mechanics of Love design courtesy of
Turner's Tokens, USA

Mousetrap by Ami Amore's
Amorticious, photography by
Insomniac Studios, USA

Design by Elease Sinister Vanity, USA

Design by Marija Jillings of Jazz Steampunk, Netherlands

Design by Marija Jillings of Jazz Steampunk, Netherlands

Ryan C. Contello Neal, photography by
Cherie Savoie, US

Zombie Dolly Lia Habel, designed by Jema Hewitt, aka Emilly Ladybird, UK

Design courtesy of Ivan Mavrovic, Croatia

Clockwork wings, designed by Jema Hewitt, aka Emilly Ladybird, UK

Watch design courtesy of Ivan Mavrovic, Croatia

Designs by Rag Dollies Madhouse, Lina Kara, Greece

Design by Rag
Dollies Madhouse,
Lina Kara, Greece

Pendant design by
Denise Humphrey, UK

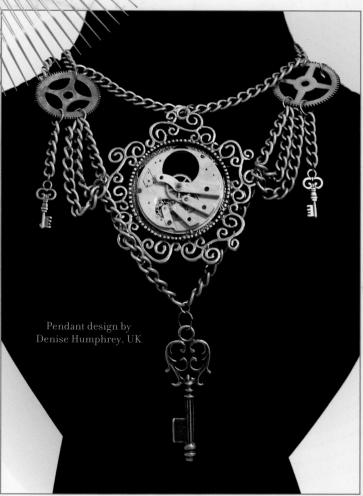

Pendant design by
Denise Humphrey, UK

Designs by Marija Jillings at Jazz Steampunk, Netherlands

Design by Rag Dollies Madhouse, Lina Kara, Greece

Peacock time piece, designed by Jema Hewitt,
aka Emilly Ladybird, UK

Pendant design by Elease Sinister Vanity, USA

Steambook, designed by Jema Hewitt, aka
Emilly Ladybird, UK

Design by Gwydyons Midnight Creations

Design by Gwydyons Midnight Creations

Rebecca Summers,
photo by Mart Soulstealer.
UK (Soulstealer.co.uk)

Designs by
Gwydyons Midnight Creations

Designs by
Gwydyons Midnight Creations

"Solar Flare," a Sightmares ™ © Bio-Mechanical
Steampunk Eye by Dr. Brassy Steamington
(www.etsy.com/shop/DrBrassysSteampunk)

Antebellum Clockworks Brass Necklace
by Dr. Brassy Steamington
(www.etsy.com/shop/DrBrassysSteampunk)

Hats by Lady Bird's Hatberdashery
(facebook.com/pages/Lady-Birds-Hatberdashery)

Skull pendant design by Elease Sinister Vanity, USA

Watch parts ring by Daniel Proulx of
Catherinette Rings, USA

Hat by Lady Bird's Hatberdashery
(facebook.com/pages/Lady-Birds-Hatberdashery)

Chapter 5
BIOGRAPHIES

MANY OF THE TALENTED PEOPLE IN THIS
BOOK SENT ME BIOGRAPHIES TO INTRODUCE
THEMSELVES. THEY ARE AS FOLLOWS:

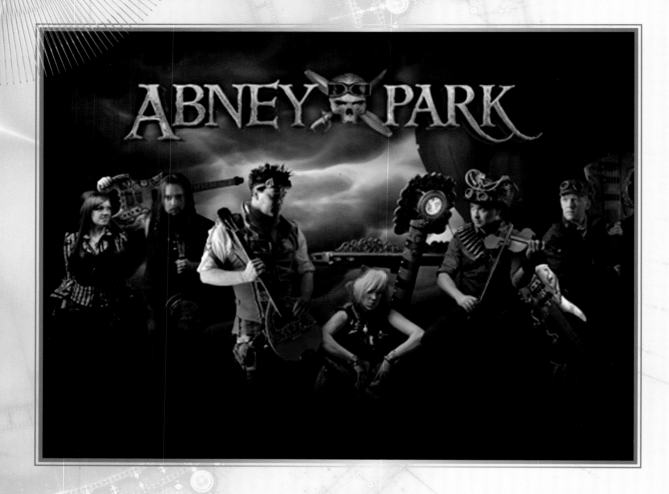

Abney Park

Abney Park comes from an era that never was, but one that we wish had been. It's an era where airships waged war in the skies and where corsets and cummerbunds were popular adventuring attire. They've picked up their bad musical habits, scoundrelous musicians, and anachronistically hybridized instruments from dozens of locations and eras that they have visited in their travels and thrown them into one riotous dervish of a performance. Expect clockwork guitars, belly dancers, flintlock bassists, Middle Eastern percussion, violent violin, and Tesla powered keyboards blazing in a post-apocalyptic swashbuckling steampunk musical mayhem. Members include Robert "Captain Robert" Brown, Kristina Erickson, Daniel Cederman, Jody Ellen, Josh Goering, and Titus Munteanu.

www.abneypark.com
www.facebook.com/pages/Abney-Park/312292093741
http://airshippirates.abneypark.com/index.html

Courtesy of Abney Park

The Artifice Club

The Artifice Club is a collection of like-minded individuals who gather together on a seasonal basis for a variety of reasons. For some, the chance to share stories of travels far and wide, or to exchange designs and plans for the latest invention gadget. For others it is a place to see and be seen by their peers and to hobnob among those of like interests. Regardless of form or desire, the club is founded as an open ground for those who have one foot in the past, one in the future, and no thought to the present. All who share the love of retro-futurism may apply, and our social events will breathe fresh life into the mundane doldrums that is the present day.

At current, we are mostly based in the southeast and have been calling Terminus (Atlanta, Georgia) our home. However, our members travel all over the world and can be found in many steampunk gatherings. We invite those who share our credo to host their own Artifice Club events or invite our members to host events at your own gathering anywhere you may live, as the proliferation of the love of a future that never was but should have been is a goal many share across the world.

THE ARTIFICE CLUB FOUNDER DOCTOR Q

Dr. Quincy Erasmus Quartermain or simply Doctor Q is an eccentric adventurer of ever increasing renown. Having a doctorate in fringe fields of theoretical philosophy and experimental engineering, his current plot to achieve mass hysteria through event production is off to a wonderful start.

He has now founded The Artifice Club as a place for those in the community of anachronists, retro-futurists, and scientists of various moral character to collect, commune, and share a drink, a story, and enjoy an entertainment or two. In addition to his skills as a Director of Musical Journeys, he is also a very well versed Master of Ceremonies and event producer. He has come highly praised from his visits of the semi-annual meeting of the Society of Morally Ambiguous Rogues and Time-Travelers (They're S.M.A.R.T!), and other such obscure organizations vouch for his skills, wit, and charm to no end, though none have gone so far as to go on record. He also takes time to pen articles and serve as the media editor for the *Steampunk Chronicle*. As if this were not enough, he serves as the senior director of arts and entertainment for the amazing steampunk and alternate history convention, Anachron.

www.theartificeclub.com
www.facebook.com/groups/ArtificeClub

Courtesy of Doctor Q of the Artifice Club, photography courtesy of Dim Horizon Studio, USA

Anthony Canney of House of Canney

The history of Savannah, the macabre of an October birth, and the pageantry of musical theatre have shaped the Vision of Anthony of The House of Canney. His passion for sewing started with doll clothing as a child, but he quickly moved on to apparel for himself and antebellum clothing for his reenacting parents by the age of 17. Anthony graduated with a BFA in media and performing arts production, which helped to polish his storytelling and color theory through fashion design. Anthony prides himself in combining pageantry and glamour with history, fantasy, and wearability.

Your Tailor,
Anthony Canney

TheHouseofCanney.com

Your source for one of a kind corsets, steampunk fashions, costumes, fantasy wear, and historic recreations.
Proud tailor to Miss Gay USofA at Large 2010, Tahjee; NEOY 2010, Vanessa Demornay; and NEOY 2009, Bianca Nicole!

And follow the Tailor on facebook for daily updates on current projects, and insights on design and fashion.

Fashions by Anthony Canney, photo courtesy of Dortch Designs, USA
Anthony Canney, photography by Thomas Dodd, USA

Veronique Chevalier

Veronique Chevalier, (aka The "Weird Val" of Dark Cabaret), is The Original Mad Sonictist, Steampunk-lish Chanteuse, Spooky Polkanista, Perv-ormance Artiste, and Authoress. One of her devotees has dubbed her "The Edith Piaf From An Alternate Reality."

Along with originals, and Piaf-ian covers of familiar tunes, she is known for her parodies on the subject of steampunk, remodeling works by Thomas Dolby, Frank Zappa, Led Zepplin, ZZ Top, and The Beatles.

The inventrix of "Gothic Polka," with the release of her recording *Polka Haunt Us: A Spook-tacular Compilation*, which MAD-emoiselle Veronique also dubs her "Sonic Franksteam," she leaves no stone unturned, nor any sacred cow unmilked, in her quest to bring levity to where the sun don't shine.

Her originals have been played on Dr. Demento Radio, Rue Morgue Radio, and the Volver a la Magia Radio-Show in Buenos Aires, among others, and her tracks can be found on numerous steampunk music compilations, including *A Sepiachord Passport* released by Projekt Records as well as *Steampunk, Vol. 1*, the Soundtrack to G.D. Falksen's novel *The Hellfire Chronicles: Blood in the Skies*.

In addition to ink in *Gothic Beauty*, *Rue Morge*, *Fangoria*, and numerous online steampunk publications, her image is included in *1000 Steampunk Creations* by Dr. Grymm. She is the 2012 recipient of the *Steampunk Chronicle's* Reader's Choice Awards for "Best Dressed Female Steampunk."

Screened as a comedy short at arts festivals and steampunk events across North America, including the Steampunk Bizarre, Seattle International Cabaret Festival, PDX Steampunk Film Festival, and S.T.E.A.M. Fest, *Internet Date* is Veronique Chevalier's gentle lampoon of the preposterous process of online courtship. With art and direction by Nickelodeon's Kyle A. Carrozza, and animation by John Berry, this winsome bit of neo-retro cartooning is certain to elicit fits of mirth, with its witty lyrics and beguiling sight gags.

The MAD-emoiselle one herself is also Creatrix of SteamKu ("Steampunk Haiku") and authoress of *My Cog Is Bigger Than Your Cog: SteamKu & Other Verstrocities*, the world's first volume of Steampunk Haiku, with full-color, retina-staining illustrations by Monsieur Walter Sickert.

Veronique Chevalier, USA

Thomas Dodd

Thomas Dodd is an Atlanta-based photographer and digital artist whose work blurs the lines between photography and classical art. His photographic images seamlessly blend the worlds of fantasy and surrealism and have been featured in magazines, on book covers, and in art galleries around the world.

For more information, please visit his website:
http://thomasdodd.com

Photography by Thomas Dodd, USA

G. D. Falksen

G. D. Falksen is an author, lecturer, public speaker, and MC. He also studies history and blogs for Tor.com. While his repertoire spans a range of topics, he is currently most noted for his steampunk work and is one of the most recognizable figures in the steampunk literary genre and the related subculture. His debut novel, *The Hellfire Chronicles: Blood in the Skies*, was released in July 2011. Other fiction includes *The Strange Case of Mr. Salad Monday*, *Cinema U*, and the serials *An Unfortunate Engagement* and *The Mask of Tezcatlipoca*. His work has appeared in *Steampunk Tales*, *Steampunk Magazine*, *The Chap*, *Egophobia*, and various anthologies such as *Footprints*, *Steampunk Reloaded*, and *The Immersion Book of Steampunk*. He has made appearances as a guest at various events, including Dragon Con, New York Comic Con, and the World Steam Expo. He has appeared in *The New York Times*, the *San Francisco Chronicle*, the *Hartford Courant*, *Marie Claire Italia*, BoingBoing.net, *Time Out New York*, and *New York Magazine*, and on MTV, NHK, VBS.tv, Space, and io9.com. He is the lead writer for AIR, a steampunk-themed video game currently in development from Hatboy Studios, Inc.

If you wish to know more, please visit his website:

www.gdfalksen.com

Left ✷ G.D. Falksen, photography by Frank Siciliano, USA

Right ✷ G.D. Falksen, photography by Lex Machina, USA

Lee Ann Farruga

Known internationally as Countessa Lenora, Canadian Queen of Steampunk, Lee Ann Farruga is the founder of Steampunk Canada, a national organization bringing together steampunks from across Canada and educating the general public about this genre and community.

A bundle of organizational energy held in check only by her impressive collection of corsets, the Countessa promotes steampunk in a plethora of venues, including the Steampunk Canada website, blogs, social media, local events, and at conventions large and small. Driven by her love of steampunk, she has brought the genre and local Canadian groups to the attention of publishers and major media companies and is campaigning to bring steampunk to the attention of all Canadians through art galleries, museums, libraries, and schools nationwide.

Lee Ann Farruga, Steampunk Canada, photography by Lex Machina

Hatton Cross Steampunk

David Lee is the principal artist at Hatton Cross Steampunk. His steampunk art was been featured in Dr. Grymm's 2011 "Steampunk Bizarre Exhibit" in the Mark Twain Museum, Connecticut. He's been a guest artist and panel presenter at numerous conventions.

His "Gentleman's Flying Apparatus," aka "The Morgan Aeronautical Destroyer of Satan's Arrogance," was nominated for "Best non-goggle accessory" in the *Steampunk Chronicle's* Readers Choice Awards. He is also a contributing "DIY" author for the *Steampunk Chronicle* website. In early 2012, David signed with publisher Ypatia Press and is due to release his first steampunk novel, *Country in Ruin–1865* later this year.

David's most recent steampunk creation is the "Gentleman's Armored Battle Carriage" (a driveable steampunk tank) which will be making numerous appearances in 2013. With all that David and Hatton Cross Steampunk have going on, they continue to push the envelope with some very ambitious projects, to include a drivable steampunk Dalek, a steampunk Séance Machine with interactive show, and numerous DIY projects for the *Steampunk Chronicle* website.

David's personal motto is "Anything worth doing is worth overdoing!" and he applies this to his steampunk creations.

www.hcsteam.net

Photography and models by Hatton Cross Steampunk, USA

Kato

Growing up in a 300-year-old rectory in Wales, with a thirteenth-century cemetery in the backyard, and parents who embraced the Victorian era set the stage for model/fashion designer Kato's love of history. Kato says, "I was presented with the perfect background and inspiration for my art and photo shoots." And what photo shoots they are!! This multimedia mogul is on fire and there's no stopping her with more than 134,000 fans on just one of her Facebook pages! She's innocently sweet and sirenly sexy, all in one package—and her fans love her. Coined the "It" girl of steampunk fashion, she is more than just a pretty face.

Kato designs some of the hottest contemporary steampunk fashions out there. She's currently working on her website, Steamgirl, which will showcase her longtime interest in highly stylized erotic photography, as well as a graphic novel, the former at the request of her fans. She has her own fashion website, Steampunk Couture, where she sells her original designs, along with a host of other merchandise avenues on Etsy—one for posters and another for her fashion line.

Originally from Britain, she moved to the United States in 2007, when she took a multimedia project in Los Angeles as a model/stylist. She now happily resides in northern Oregon. It seems that fashion has always been in her blood. At age 11 she was sketching fashions. After a few years, and six broken sewing machines later, she began sewing her own clothes. This self-taught seamstress was discovered when a former band member of Abney Park remarked how steampunk her designs were. That year she took a chance and started her own business, never to look back.

What does Kato love most about steampunk? In her own words, "It's the perfect marriage of the two aesthetics I've always adored most and it covers so many areas of life that you're immersed in. There are also no rules, so the stylistic possibilities are endless, and as a designer I find this very exciting."

Stay tuned for more amazing things from this steampunk phenomenon…

www.steampunkcouture.com

WWW.STEAMGIRL.COM • WWW.ETSY.COM/SHOP/STEAMPUNKCOUTURE • WWW.FACEBOOK.COM/STEAMPUNKCOUTURE • WWW.FACEBOOK.COM/STEAMPUNKATO • WWW.ETSY.COM/SHOP/KATOMERCH

Kato

P.O. Box 1904, Sandy, OR 97055, USA

Evelyn Kriete

Evelyn Kriete is an editor, artist, fashion designer, marketing adviser, and promoter with ten years of active experience in events organization and marketing. Along with being an event producer with active involvement in a wide range of subcultures and trends, she is known as the major steampunk organizer in New York, a principle organizer worldwide, and a moving force behind the steampunk trend. She has worked closely with various reporters, researchers, and media outlets during their coverage of steampunk, including but not limited to *The New York Times*, MTV, NHK, VBS.tv, NBC, and the *San Francisco Chronicle*. She does programming and staff work for Dragon Con, NYCC, and other major conventions.

She co-produces Dorian's Parlor, Phildaelphia's premier monthly black tie event. She provides media and networking services for numerous artists the world wide. She is the co-founder of Gilded Age Records, the first ever steampunk music label; she is also the co-founder of the Annual Time Travel Picnic, the oldest annual steampunk meet up event.

Her art has appeared in numerous art shows across the country and in a range of publications. She moderates the Steamfashion community and blogs for Brass Goggles as well for Tor.com. She has previously worked with various projects such as *Repo! The Genetic Opera*, the steampunk exhibition at the Museum of the History of Science in Oxford, and *Make* Magazine's World Maker Faire New York. She is currently working with a number of film projects and TV shows, including *The Marionette Unit* and *War of the Worlds: Goliath*. She also works with *Weird Tales* magazine. She is the creative director for *Steampunk Tales* magazine and the editor of Wildside Press' forthcoming *Steampunk Classics* line of books.

Her writing has appeared in books such as *Steampunk Reloaded* and will be appearing in seven different books due out over the course of the next two years, including the forthcoming *Steampunk Bible*. She is also the Marketing Director for Hatboy Studios's forthcoming video game "AIR: Steampunk." She is a fashion designer for the Australian clothing label Galley Serpentine. Evelyn has been the principle stylist for numerous photo shoots and the producer of more fashion shows than she can count. It is said that she does, in fact, sleep and eat, but to date the claims are merely rumors. She is also very excited to have a hat named after her by Topsy Turvy Design.

Evelyn Kriete wearing the officers coat worn in the film *Wild Wild West*, a blouse from Retroscope Fashion, and a hat—"The Evelyn" from Topsy Turvy Designs

League of S.T.E.A.M.
The League of S.T.E.A.M. is not your average performance group.

Our talented group of inventors and actors take the audience back to a time of scientific adventure, a common ground between the paranormal and the Pythagorean. We are monster hunters from the Victorian era. From up on the stage to mingling the crowd, our members engage the audience with proton packs capable of firing blasts of steam, zombie man servants on chain leads, net guns and titillating electro-shock packs, and ethereal glowing ghosts. Every piece of machinery is meticulously designed, detailed, and fully functional, from the steam cannon to the extendable Punch Fist. The League travels with an archive of past adventures, preserved and documented for the ambient pleasure of the viewer, featuring exotic specimens and chilling relics from the ancient Orient. Audiences for this extravagant experience continue to grow. The League of S.T.E.A.M. is one of the fastest growing entertainment groups of its kind, and our series of filmed exploits has insured us a popularity that fills our events to capacity. And now I give you The League of S.T.E.A.M...

All League of Steam photography by Greg De Stefano, USA

Crackitus Potts
Non-Lethal Specialist
Co-Founder

Specializing in non-lethal weapons and equipment, Crackitus Potts' cleverly-engineered gadgets aid him in capturing and incapacitating all manner of supernatural creatures. His arsenal may seem innocuous, but assisted by the tremendous power of steam, electricity, and kinetics, he can be a formidable opponent. Additionally, he utilizes his advanced steam-powered apparition apprehension apparatus to eradicate ectoplasmic entities (after all, it's not lethal if they're already dead!)

Baron Von Fogel
Zombie Exterminator

Baron von Fogel is devoted to abolishing the incessant menace of the living dead which plague our society. Armed with his hand-cranked chainsaw and trusty machete, the Baron serves to make the world a better place, one headless zombie at a time.

Lady Ameliorette Potts
Tactical Coordination Specialist
Co-Founder

When the League finds itself in a troublesome spot (as is too frequently the case), Lady Potts is undoubtedly the one who will fix the situation!

Sir Conrad Wright III
Vampire Elimination Specialist

Sir Conrad enjoys long strolls in darkened cemeteries, where he uses his unique assortment of sharp pointy objects to exterminate the Unholy Undead and speed up nature's process of decomposition. Known to many colleagues simply as "Vampire Hunter C," Sir Conrad wields a deadly arsenal of weaponry. Beware of his garlic soufflé if you have an aversion to holy objects or the sun.

JayAre
Ectoplasmic Auditory Tracking Specialist
Co-Founder

Recently a disciple of Thomas Edison, this chap, who goes simply by JR, joined the League following his turbulent downfall with Edison Industries. Serving as tracking expert for the team, JR excels in monitoring electronic voice phenomena and other supernatural evidence.

Katherine Blackmoore
Undead Pulverizer

Ms. Blackmoore is contracted by the League of S.T.E.A.M. on a regular basis to aid in their efforts to reduce the population of the living dead. An expert with blunt objects, she favors baseball and cricket bats as her primary skull-crushing weapons.

Jasper Mooney
Lycanthrope Disposal Specialist

Jasper Mooney is dedicated to an unceasing quest to ferret out and abrogate lycanthropes, and he has honed his seeking, searching, and stalking skills to a keen edge. These uncanny abilities, coupled with advanced steam propulsion theory and cinnabar-driven contrivances, render all lycanthropic entities harmless and hairless.

Thaddeus
Gentleman's Gentleman to the League

Alpha to his twin brother Zeddediah & #039;s Omega, Thaddeus is tireless in his assistance to the League. When not pressing the linens or preparing Mr. Potts a cocktail, Thaddeus scours the globe for the rare and unusual botanical compounds that are the essential ingredients to his infusions. He hopes that one day he will discover the combination that will cure his twin's condition.

Zeddediah
Gentleman's Gentleman to the League

A tireless and dedicated servant, assistant, valet, and confidant to Mr. Potts and company, Zeddediah is one half of a dedicated duo. By relieving the League of distracting day-to-day worries and allowing them to focus on their innovations and the containment of supernatural plagues of mankind, the twins have proven to be an integral part of the team.

The Russian
Cryptozoological Expert

The Russian is *the* go-to source for any and all information pertaining to mythological, cryptozoological, and biological creatures that inhabit our world or any plane attached to it. She found that joining the League suits her research needs, as their activities grant her greater exposure to the super and extra-natural creatures of which she studies than she could manage solo. The Russian's secretive nature and mysterious past belies a tender heart that cannot resist helping the creatures she comes across.

Coyote
League of S.T.E.A.M. Liaison
W.A.T.C.H. Co-Founder

Ellie Copperbottom
League of S.T.E.A.M. Liaison
W.A.T.C.H. Co-Founder

After moving into the house next to the League of S.T.E.A.M. & #039;s Manor with Ellie Copperbottom, the jovial and inquisitive Coyote quickly established a friendly bond between the houses. Upon noticing how the League was struggling with the world's surplus of paranormal activity, Ellie and Coyote founded the Worldwide Alliance for the Tracking of Creatures and Haunts (W.A.T.C.H.) to collect and compile reports from around the world. Coyote also has an uncanny ability with the League's field equipment, even though no one can remember training him on it...

Ellie would much rather stay at home baking then go out on adventures with "the boys." Ellie and Coyote could not help but become aware of the League's (mis)adventures. After a particularly... unpleasant...mishap with a kitten in a tree, they decided to create the League W.A.T.C.H. (Worldwide Alliance for the Tracking of Creatures and Haunts) in order to help the S.T.E.A.M. League (and guard against future kitty killings!) While Ellie is resourceful and fully capable of defending herself, her best defense is to avoid conflict and bake some nice warm chocolate chip cookies!

Special thanks to Russell Isler for providing this information.
For more information about the League, please visit:
http://leagueofsteam.com

Pierre Leszczyk

ROMANTICISM AND MELANCHOLY:
Pierre Leszczyk, the modern Caspar David Friedrich of photography

The photographer Pierre Leszczyk's works (EmpireArt) are characterized by sophisticated staging, historically inspired costumes, and an expression of desire. If you take a look at the results of his work you will see him as the modern Caspar David Friedrich of photography. With his style of pictures Leszczyk presents a completely new interpretation of romanticism and melancholy (www.walimex.com).

"I wish to wake a very special desire in people with my photography, making them dive right in by taking them on a modern type of time travel. Personally, I travel a lot across the 'Old Europe:' Venice, Florence, Prague, Dresden, Antwerp, etc. They are wonderful destinations; their historical backdrop inspires me. On my last summer holiday I sat close to the Piazza della Signoria in Florence and painted Michelangelo's *David*. That kind of intense moment is remembered for a very long time since it leaves an imprint on my soul.

"Italy's monumental cemeteries are also full of spirituality. This is where you will find beautiful marble sculptures that embody strong emotions. I draw the fantasy for my shoots from these impressions and experiences. This year, several historical balls are on my travelling agenda, as is the Carnival of Venice. I am happy to see that the public interest in events with such an exciting historical context is increasing. In particular, I am fascinated with the times around 1900, in connection with Jules Verne's books and the resulting steampunk movement which is very popular today.

"However, to me, one of 2010's absolute highlights was the visit by the Focus TV team that accompanied me at one of my shoots in July. The story of the shoot was based on a historical vampire story which you can read about in detail on my website at www.pierre-leszczyk.com. The shoot itself took place at the baroque Castle of Bad Arolsen."

Left ✷ Photography and modeling by Pierre Leszczyk EmpireArt, Germany

Right ✷ Maan Limburg and Kevin Timmerman, designs by Rosie's Art, photography by Pierre Leszczyk EmpireArt, Germany

Jon Magnificent

Jon Magnificent is a multiple award-winning steampunk recording artist who has performed at many of the west coast steampunk conventions such as Wild Wild West Con, Gaslight Gathering, Nova Albion, and Her Royal Majesty's Steampunk Symposium aboard the Queen Mary in Long Beach, California. His awards include: Orchestral Composer of the Year (2008), Rock Album of the Year (2010), Rock Artist of the Year (2011), and International Steampunk Band of the Year (2011).

Jon Magnificent and Bobbie Magnificent at the L. A. Music Awards, photography by Nelson Shen, USA

The Men That Will Not Be Blamed For Nothing

Formed in 2008 by Andrew O'Neill and Andy Heintz, The Men That Will Not Be Blamed For Nothing have been featured on the cover of the lifestyle magazine *The Chap*, within the covers of *Bizarre* Magazine and *NME*, and have played in diverse venues including comedy clubs, festivals, and theatres (the latter in support of front man O'Neill on the tour of his comedy show *Andrew O'Neill's Totally Spot On History of British Industry*).

Their debut album, entitled *Now That's What I Call Steampunk! Volume 1* was released on the 24th of May, 2010. In May 2010, original drummer Ben Dawson departed and was replaced with Jez Miller, formerly of Showgirls and Lords of the New Church. A special limited edition 7" EP entitled *A Very Steampunk Christmas EP*, was released on the 6th of December, 2010, featuring the new lineup. An exclusive limited edition live album was recorded at Nambucca, Holloway Road, London, UK entitled *Anachrony in the UK Live in London* in April 2011, and was released on the 28th of May, 2011.

Andy Heintz & The Men That Will Not Be Blamed For Nothing, photography courtesy of T.P. Sutton (facebook.com/blamedfornothing), UK

JeniViva Mia

JeniViva Mia was a theatrical fusion belly dance artist, teacher, writer, creator, and conjurer of all things magickal and lovely. She was one of the East Coast pioneers of the Gothic Bellydance movement and director and choreographer for the Mystical Hips Theatrical Fusion Bellydance Tribe, with deep roots in Turkish cabaret, Tribal Fusion, and Spanish-Arabic fusion bellydance, as well as method acting.

She created her own headpieces, many with a steampunk design. JeniViva submitted these photos of some of her recent creations to be included in this book. She wrote, "I am attaching a recent photo of some headpieces that I made for the Steampunk Soiree in New Orleans. After seeing all the steampunk designs I went crazy and started making steampunk inspired ones."

Author's note: She will be greatly missed by all who knew and loved her. JeniViva Mia passed away in November 2011while this book was still in production. Her loving mother Annette has given permission to honor JeniViva so that her radiance will never be forgotten. It's an honor for me to include her in this book.

Top left ✳ By Pixie Vision Productions

Top center ✳ By German photographer Starkall

Top right ✳ In Moulon Rouge shoot by German photographer Starkall

Bottom center ✳ Headpieces, courtesy of JeniViva Mia, USA

Cris Ortega

Cris Ortega was born in Valladolid, Spain, in 1980 and took an interest in art and literature since she was a child—with a special love for the horror genre. Although it was a great hobby for her, she wanted to study aeronautics or astronomy as a career. It was in 1999 when she drew her first comic about one of the short stories she had written and from that moment on she began to work seriously on this profession.

While she was studying as superior technician of illustration in the Art School of Valladolid, she began to publish her work on fanzines, in magazines, and with publishers out of Spain, working at the same time as a drawing teacher and exposing her work at several exhibitions. When she finished her art studies she worked for several years as art director at the advertising agency Sm2, spending her free time making commissions, book covers, and an edition of the comic anthology, *Shade*.

At the end of 2005, she began work as an illustrator for Norma Editorial, where one and a half years later she published her first book of written stories, *Forgotten*, an art book series with several volumes. Three of them have already been published and translated in several languages. During all of her years in the profession she has worked in several fields, from graphic design and advertising to design of figures and games, concept art, role playing, video games, comics, photography, cover design, and logos. In her free time she likes to travel, read, write, and photograph landscapes. She also studies archeology, history, and astronomy.

Her most recent artworks have been published in well-known art books such as *Exotique* and *Spectrum*, and produced for many products and games. She has also had many exhibitions.

Courtesy of artist Cris Ortega, Spain

Daniel Proulx
of Catherinette Rings

Daniel Proulx was born in Montreal and spent a considerable time travelling the world before returning to his artistic roots, becoming an independent artist in 2008. He has found great inspiration in the steam era and now makes steampunk jewelry with metal wire, gemstones, vintage clock parts, and other unusual components. He loves creating organic shapes from wire and developing intricate designs with a mechanical/industrial feel. When Daniel was little he used to daydream about fantastic imaginary worlds. He would draw monsters, invent stories about magical items, or role-play with friends. Now he brings his art to life with stories from a distant, parallel steampunk universe. He uses his creations to share his passion for the world of steampunk with the rest of us.

His jewelry is available on ETSY at
www.etsy.com/shop/CatherinetteRings

Daniel Proulx Steampunk Jewelry, Robot Ring—copper reptile taxidermy glass eye artifact, featured daily deviation on DeviantArt, USA

Tie tack with reptile eye

Graf Starkall

Starkall is a writer and photographer from Prussia, the heartland of Germany. He studied Germanic theurgy, the law, and a few other absurd academics. A few of his images were published in the United States recently. Most of the time Starkall is travelling the world looking to meet new challenges, old spooks, and everlasting beauty. He is the infamous creator of Preußen Punk and a stalwart of a few other legal (more or less) preferences. Nobody knows exactly where he makes his money, but some guess he is working part time in a high security asylum and stealing their best ideas for his stories. Is it insane? Sure!

Photography by Pierre Leszczyk EmpireArt, Germany

Martin Soulstealer

Soulstealer Photography began life in the vampire/goth/alt scene in London several years ago, documenting the unique and beautifully creative people who frequented the darkest corners of the capital. Steampunk bubbled to the surface with a Vampires vs. Steampunks event: Soulstealer took the side of the 'punks and never looked back. Brown is the new black.

For more information:
Soulstealer.co.uk

Photography by Mart Soulstealer, UK (Soulstealer.co.uk)

Thomas Willeford
(aka Lord Featherstone)
BRUTE FORCE STUDIOS

With degrees in physics, history, and art, it was perhaps inevitable that Thomas Willeford (aka Lord Archibald "Feathers" Featherstone) would become a steampunk enthusiast. His work blurs the precarious line between art and engineering. If, upon viewing a piece, one does not ask "Does that actually work?" he considers the piece a failure.

Thomas has been creating unique and beautiful corsets and all manner of striking steampunk gadgetry for more than 20 years. He and his products have been widely featured on television (MTV, BBC, *Castle*, *Oddities*), online (*Wired*, BoingBoing, *Popular Mechanics*, *Playboy* TV), and in print (Art Donovan's *The Art of Steampunk*, Morgan Spurlock and Stan Lee's *Comic Con Episode IV: A Fan's Hope*, *Bizarre* magazine, *Hustler* magazine, *Gothic Beauty Magazine*, *Marquis* magazine, *Leg Show* magazine, *Pirates Magazine*, *DDI* magazine, *Culture Asylum Magazine*). Satisfied customers include David Silverman (*The Simpsons*), Patricia Tallman (*Babylon 5*), Virginia Hey (*Farscape*), and bands Abney Park, Ghostfire, and Beautiful Deadly Children. Thomas also contributed to the design of Alchemy Gothic's "Empire Collection," a line of steampunk jewelry and accessories.

Thomas' artwork has also been featured in numerous museum exhibitions worldwide, including Penn State's "STEAMpunk!," Dr. Grymm's "Steampunk Bizarre," the Charles River Museum of Industry and Innovation's "Steampunk: Form and Function," the Ashmolean Museum of the History of Science at Oxford's "Steampunk," "20,000 Leagues" at Patriot Place, and "Mobilis in Mobili" at The Wooster Street Social Club (home of TLC's NY Ink). His clockwork spider "Arachnae Mechanica" is currently housed in the Cosmopolitan Hotel in Las Vegas, Nevada.

www.bruteforcestudios.com
www.facebook.com/groups/328157016906
Twitter: @BForceStudios

Photo by Rudebwoy Photos

Chapter 6

STEAMPUNK FASHION
RESOURCES & ORGANIZATIONS

This list is not all-inclusive, there are thousands of great sites on the Internet which you can search for yourself. Here are a few to get you started:

STEAMPUNK CLOTHING AND ACCESSORIES SOURCES

artfire.com/ext/marketplace/trends/
steampunk
Blanchesplace.com
Blueladycouture.co.uk
Bruteforceleather.com
Bustledress.com
Buysteampunk.com
Chrononautmercantile.com
Clockworkbutterfly.net
Clockworkcouture.com
Markcordory.com
Darkgarden.com
Datamancer.net
Dortchdesigns.com
etsy.com/shop/catherinetterings
Etsy.com/shop/gwydyon
Etsy.com/shop/indigolights
Etsy.com/shop/RagDolliesMadhouse
Etsy.com/shop/ReactionDesigns
Etsy.com/shop/SinisterVanity
Etsy.com/people/SparkleyJem
etsy.com/shop/steambaby
Etsy.com/shop/steampunksurplus
Etsy.com/people/thesunandtheturtle
Etsy.com/shop/timeinfantasy
Etsy.com/shop/VooDooBunny
Facebook.com/Jazzsteampunk
Facebook.com/mirzhin.creation
Facebook.com/TurnersTokens

Facebook.com/pages/VeeCee-Design-
Co/124201257616418?fref=ts
Ivan Mavrovic designs: http://mental-
design.blogspot.com
Museumreplicas.com/s-50-steampunk.
aspx
Premierclothing.com
Pyramidcollection.com
Ragdollpunx.daportfolio.com
Recollections.biz
Retroscopefashions.com
Rocklove.com/falksen-fox
Spankyspanglerdesign.co.uk
Steambaby.net
Steamedpunk.com
Steampunkemporium.com
Steampunkthreads.com
Sutlers.co.uk
TheHouseOfCanney.com
TurnersTokens.com
VeeCeeDesigns.com
VeilOfVisions.com

Other fine steampunk sites, photographers, and organizations include:

Adavidphotography.com
Beyondvictoriana.com
Brassgoggles.co.uk/blog
Cheriesavoie.com/photography
Crisortega.com
Doriansparlor.com
www.Empireart.de
FrankSiciliano.com

GdFalksen.com
Gdfalksen.com/bloodintheskies
Gdfoto.com
Insomniacstudios.net
Jaborwhalky.net
Facebook.com/pages/Artist-Josh-
Stebbins
Facebook.com/blamedfornothing
Facebook.com/neave.r.willoughby
JerryAbuan.Zenfolio.com
JohnThomasGrant.com
Leagueofsteam.com
Lexmachinaphoto.com
Modelmayhem.com/1306382
Myspace.com/bbblackdoguk
Nbpix-photographie.com
Pauldoyle@photographybypaul.com
Pixievisionproductions.com
Randomeyecandy.com
RayFeatherphotography.com
Scott.read@imp-net.co.uk
Starkall.de/v2
Steamfashion.livejournal.com/profile
Steampunkcanada.ca/
Steampunkchronicle.com
Steampunkitalia.com
Steampunktales.com/
Stevenrosenphotography.com
Soulstealer.co.uk
TheArtificeClub.com
Gildedagerecords.com/
TheGoldenGear.foroactivo.net/
Thomasdodd.com
tor.com/blogs/2009/10/steampunk-101
Turner-photo.com
Warped-prod.com
WeirdVal.com

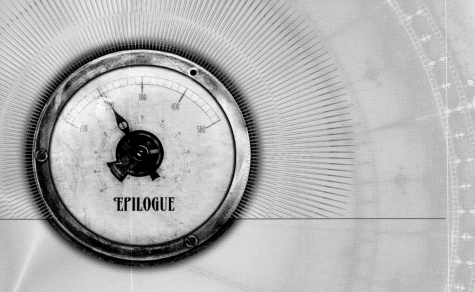

EPILOGUE

This is the end of the book, but not the end for steampunk. It is just the beginning as more people are drawn to its old-world charm and manners…I look forward to watching it unfold and feel a rare privilege to have been a part of conveying the message, even in a small way.

Kindest regards,
Victoriana Lady Lisa, author and historian

VictorianaLady.com
Victorianaladylisa.blogspot.com
To contact the author, e-mail Lisa@Victorianalady.com